Another lovely talent! With best wishes, Annie, for Christmas and the New Year, congratulations on building such a good school and thanks for our long and stimulating friendship. Love David 2004.

TROUBLE IN THE HEARTLAND

Trouble in the Heartland

JOEL LANE

PUBLICATIONS
2004

Published by Arc Publications
Nanholme Mill, Shaw Wood Road
Todmorden OL14 6DA, UK

© Joel Lane 2004

Design by Tony Ward
Print by Antony Rowe Ltd.,
Eastbourne, East Sussex

ISBN 1 900072 99 8

Cover design by Tony Ward

Thanks are due to the editors of the magazines and
anthologies in which some of these poems first appeared:
*Pretext, The Rialto, Scratch, Thumbscrew, Poetry London,
Other Poetry, The Interpreter's House, Leviathan,
Headlock, Times Literary Supplement, Talebones,
Poetry Wales, Rain Dog, Reactions, Liar Inc,
Smiths Knoll, Obsessed With Pipework, Seam, The North.*

Thanks are also due to the following for their help,
advice and encouragement:
Cannon Poets, Tony Charles, Dad, Gul Davis, David Hart,
John Howard, Angela Jarman, Helen Kitson,
Michael Mackmin, Ian McMillan, Chris Morgan,
David Morley, Mum, Kate Pearce, Deryn Rees-Jones,
Mark Robinson, Nick Royle, Sibyl Ruth, Mick Scully,
Sarah Snashall, Elly Tams, Tony Ward, Frances Wilson.

The Publishers acknowledge financial
assistance from ACE Yorkshire

Editor for UK / Ireland: Jo Shapcott

For Gul Davis,
a poet of solitude

and in memory of
John Lane
(1940-2003)

Contents

3 COMMON GROUND

HARD COPY

Heartland

It doesn't move, but it turns.
So gradually, you don't know
if it's you or the world going round.
And it breathes. You're trapped under it.
So you leave. The wind pushes you
and everything is streamlined: time,
daylight, career, talk. The centre
is a bad dream you sweat at night,
take paracetamol for. But
somewhere inside you, the needle
is still turning, broken. It's
the Northness of these houses
that furs up your hollow bones.
The Southness of these people
that makes your feet itch.
Who needs your profile anyway?
And tonight a train carries you,
like water in a pail. There.
There are voices in the dark,
and the city sifting traffic
like some underground monster
stirring, the ocean dragging fossils
through sand. You're asleep
before you've even stopped thinking.

Letters Page

Trapped in the mist of a net curtain,
he looks out at decline. His dogs
leave piss trails like question marks
in the thinning snow. His eye
for an eye admits no small change.

Thaw or no thaw, he's not giving
an inch. Beyond the celluloid walls
children have smoked the garden bare.
His skin has turned to dry paper,
stained pink at the edges.

The street consumes each dropped coin,
hoards its own past sayings,
breathes the carbon monoxide
of publicity on every blurred snapshot.
It's all too simple for words, yet

too complex to be understood.
Even small-talk is karaoke
when everyone speaks with a Local Voice.
Snow drifts between the columns, where
dummy copy rots into meaning.

The April winds shake the tiny
world like a glass paperweight,
and the black flakes settle down again
to ruin the sheets on the washing line,
like always. Trust is a joke.

Station

The snow was coming down fast and soft,
but the roadway was still visible
when the last taxi pulled out of town
and the shivering queues around the station

waited, argued about it, then broke
apart to look for telephones.
By three a.m. they were drifting
like fingers on a silent keyboard.

And the slow paper-chase went on
with a strange calmness, the lost
hiding somewhere inside themselves
as if they were trapped in a screen

between light and dark, and the last reel
might annihilate their thin lives,
and the razors in the air might cut
their throats to delicate ribbons.

The streets had never seen such a lack
of violence. Two boys were kissing
in full view, like getting your head
kicked in was an urban myth.

The dreaming city gathered its thoughts
into the train station, where couples
took turns to share the half-sleep
of an embrace in a photo-booth,

and a hundred nightclub refugees
sat in the waiting room, an audience
for some film even older than this –
until five, when they stumbled out

to where the darkness lay on a bed
of clotted light, and the first buses came
like mammoths rising from the ice age,
bearing silent passengers out to sleep.

The Grand Hotel

The August heatwave has come back.
The crossword of paths around the cathedral
is filled in by dazzled youngsters.

In a backstreet just off Colmore Row
I'm looking for a small exhibition
of photos of Dylan from 1969.

In a doorway by the Grand Hotel
a boy is sleeping in a blanket roll,
the sun glowing on his pale face.

The photos show Dylan in role
as husband and father, The Band
awkward in their Civil War suits.

As I walk back, the police
are arresting the boy, his possessions
crammed into a grey bin liner –

and I stop in the hotel's shadow
with a line of The Band's in my head:
the crime of having nowhere to go.

Neo

The city is melting like fat.
There are faces in the paving-stones
and the wires of rain tighten
and vibrate, a thousand chords;

the bassline pours into the hall
to feed the crowd whose voice
lifts the singer, like a dark wave.
And tonight, never mind the date,

someone has spiked the city's drink:
the dead town is fading, the town
where the fist showed its bony face
on the edge of every district

and the air stung every new throat.
The ghosts are silent. Tonight
the city is melting into rain,
into music, into a different life.

Wolverhampton, December 2000

The Birmingham Surrealists

woke up in a foul temper
because of the seals barking
on the telegraph wires

threw bags of cod and chips
into the city reservoir
and fished them back out

were totally unimpressed
by the election promises
of the four skeletal horsemen

occupied the number 11 bus
singing *Keep right on*
to the end of the circle

painted their faces gold
before deciding that it just
wasn't the right weather for it

got drunk on Venusian Mild
and pissed a meteor shower
over the local allotments

went out secretly at night
to run a cosmic steamroller
over the world's vowels

fucked up, surprising no-one
but raising their profile
among the glass community

Soho Hill

Under the shallow curve of the flyover,
skateboarders dodge invisible barriers
and pigeons scrape fragments of naan.
The shadow follows you to the hilltop,
then burns like oil in the silver flame
of the new Sikh temple. Stone crests
shimmer as if primed to short-circuit.

Ten years ago, these shops displayed
cheap groceries and dried-out roots;
the upper windows were boarded.
Now, the street is a living catalogue:
imported clothes and fabrics, music,
videos, books. The eyes of the economy
are dazzled by every kind of light.

Among the new facades, a few blank
shells remain, half-dressed in posters.
Teenagers drift hastily from door
to door, unwilling to be framed.
Their parents keep their eyes on the road.
They know what all this was built on,
what it has cost, what it still might.

Greet

It's not about temperature, this cold.
There's something falling, only just visible;
it's not snow, hardly even sleet.
It's the glass from the new phone box
that didn't last the weekend.

It's the torn breath of the children
who ask for a coin, then snatch your change.
It's the fading cries from the back yard
where the lovers shiver and catch their deaths
of anything but cold. It's the rotten fruit

in a stone jar, the smell of that.
It's the spent whisper of credit cards.
By the traffic island, there's a poster
showing a toilet door that someone
has marked with shit. The poster, I mean.

Outside the video shop, a pale stranger
asks, *You seen my boyfriend?* You say no.
She snaps back, *Liar.* It's the ignored
news: distant violence, global warming
accelerating the schedule of ice.

Retro

It's all coming back:
reggae, boy bands, long hair,
the Cold War, ska, heroin
and blood on the pavement.

Hello again to the man
with a swastika armband
calling on the Dunkirk spirit,
hello again to the mob
who can't see the contradiction.

Stale language, broken up,
reheated and foil-wrapped,
the only way it makes sense.
Hello again to the spoon
feeding words into empty mouths.

But the blood on the pavement
has no shades of meaning,
has only its dull fire
to stain the city streets
like a sticker tattoo,
a retro synthetic birthmark.

Poison Road

The hive is shaking like a sore head.
The army are on the road again,
out into the stingable world –
sucking the nectar from its fruits,

laying white eggs in rotten wood,
showing off their pointed behinds
striped by the good healthy birch;
mouths full of pulp and rumour,

eyes bigger than their bellies,
poison sacs bigger than either;
laying down the venom tracks,
shivering in a foreign wind,

knocking back neat gin and lemon,
farting death in a fever storm;
wearing the iron mask of duty
to deliver their cold injection,

the slow jets of the officer's mess.
There's only one road on the map.
Back in the papier-mâché barracks,
they're breaking up their homeland

into model colonies, cutting out lines
of poison across the dry tarmac;
crouching behind the door, a finger
scraping the rust from a loaded gun.

Newspaper Soup

You can leave your baggage at the port.
All that history. The burnt papers,
the face-effect shrouds. We know better.
We don't even believe our own fears

unless it suits us. It's a game.
Asking questions to poke the scars:
Were you tortured? How much?
How many of your family were killed?

And the bottom line: *Have you truly*
suffered enough to merit the fuck all
we have to offer? Our blue-veined bread?
Our bowls of tasteless newspaper soup?

The Turin Video

When they stormed the derelict station
where the Beast had his lair,
they found a map of the world
with everywhere marked for invasion,

and books on electrical science
printed in an unknown language,
and a dusty videocassette left
at the bottom of a wooden chest.

It showed the false prophet
gloating as he described how he'd
duped his followers into acts
that had made the world shudder.

With the smirk of the Grinch
he enacted a silent mock prayer,
then wrapped himself in a cloak
of invisibility. That was all.

A trail of rumour and dust
led his pursuers across the world.
Bombs fell like a curtain.
Footage taken by the CIA

showed his tall silhouette riding
the back of a winged dinosaur.
His body was never recovered.
But in the ruins of some country

or other, a charred journal came
to light. Experts verified his hand,
his voice: a mixture of delusion
and propaganda, a fallen text.

Master

You were never the one who belonged.
New boy who was slow to learn,
they whispered about your parents
and laughed at your sad clothes.
You used fear to make new friends,
got them to do your hurting for you.

Soon the playground was your domain,
its invisible boundaries mapped out
with required tributes, blood and skin.
You taught them flesh, made them suffer
as men and women before puberty.
They'd never be the same again.

You hoarded their tears like money.
But for all your calculated rage,
your greed for bribes and piss-stains,
the penny never dropped: you were blind
to the tax that would be paid, the fire
promised to your name, your home, your children.

Read My Lips

'There will be dancing in the streets
when we liberate the city.'

But when we entered the city
there was no dancing.
There were no feet to dance,
no streets to dance in.
And in the scorched rubble
the only thing standing
was the flag we planted.

To drown out the mournful wind
we gave flags to a few survivors
and ordered them to chant 'freedom',
so the footage could be shown
in all of our broadcasts.

But in the desert nations
they played the tape backwards
with no soundtrack,
and lip-read the word 'murder'.

Metal

As the occupying force
put down each new uprising,
its politicians brought out
the same shiny phrase:

Winning their hearts and minds.
It became shorthand: *We're going
in with Cruise hearts and minds
missiles.* After six months

it was a raw shred of meaning:
*Body count patriot napalm
hearts and minds brick dust teeth.*
Still the words kept rattling out

like coins from a one-armed bandit:
heats and minds gathered up
hearts and minds like handfuls
of loose *hearts and minds* change,

their only sense a flavour
of tarnished copper, of blood
and verdigris, something almost
as cheap as human life.

The Disbelievers

They live in houses with no keys,
glare at the world over a pint
that never gets them drunk.

When the mermaids sing to them
from the wounded shell of dawn,
they check the shipping forecast.

It's so tiresome, that botched wall
of doubt, all mortar and no bricks;
that whining, undermining *Sure*.

Yet, without it, the sea of faith
would storm in a black glossy tide
through every window and screen,

the light of belief be the flash
before the howling of thunder,
the landslip, the gullible rain.

I give thanks each day for unbelief,
the gift of the sceptics; but really,
you wouldn't want to know them.

Off the Record

The new railway timetable
is up on the station wall
behind a sheet of perspex.
But the new lines aren't ready,

so the timetable has reverted
to the one now out of print:
a schedule that only exists
in the memories of passengers.

Sometimes we forget, and the lines
remain empty. Late at night,
a solitary drunk catches
the same train over and over.

Solo Flight

White Label

The way I feel breaks copyright. For weeks
I've been saving up your best lines
to echo in my head, the way
the moon echoes daylight.
It feels like I've swallowed a window.

These ghosts of your face, your voice,
your smile, aren't approved by you.
I've bootlegged them from stray moments,
distilled them, like moonshine
spirit in a white-labelled bottle

or an illicit remix on a club disc.
A moonlight operation. Your strobe
drains me. I'm a screen, a page.
Every day I try to hide from it.
Whenever I speak I say your name.

The old story: I can make you laugh,
but I can't make you happy.
I've given you the keys to a car
you don't want to drive or ride in.
You can leave it to rust in the alley

or push it, empty, over a cliff.
The sunlight feels so cold. Just like
last night, when the moon opened
every door in the house, and left me
shivering in its gentle absence.

Take My Hand

Coming back late from a wedding,
the car twisted on one wheel
and broke through a low hedge
before slamming into the brick wall

that crumpled like a sheet of paper.
They were all cousins of the bride,
the three men in the car. The driver
was the youngest by a few years.

According to the coroner, he'd drunk
more than the others. Had a history.
They should never have let him drive.
But they did. It's hard to see

who was really in charge.
On the empty seat was a map
folded to the wrong place, a streak
of blood wiping out a town.

What Happened To You?

Don't show me your objectivity
like a new pair of cufflinks.
Don't show me your new cufflinks.
Don't wave your plastic in my face
like a passport without a photo.
Don't give me that knowing look.

Tell me how you couldn't find
your way home in broad daylight.
How your fist cracked like a stone
and you saw the ocean within it.
How you were a father for a week
and a baby for a long weekend.

Or tell me about going to vote
and leaving the card unmarked.
How you watched a swastika drag
its broken legs up a wall.
How the open face of a country
closed and shrank like scar tissue.

But don't give me a balanced opinion
when the truth is off balance.
Don't answer your own questions
by flicking conjectural ash
from a cigarette you've given up.
Don't confuse reason with this.

Carousel

Election weather. Too bright to see clearly;
rain waking you up in the night.
All your feelings come back at once

in a cluster, like a manifesto
with no sense of history: a rose
made up of petals from other flowers.

A dream informs you about love.
The paper men are everywhere, touching
flesh to make themselves real,

flattering the guilty and damning
the innocent with faint praise.
The soundbites are closing on your head;

there's a stillness beneath, a May
where all your betrayals lie in wait.
They toil not, neither do they spin.

The Black Window

When the last film had ended,
sometimes, he'd sit in the dark
with a glass in his hand, and watch.

Himself, a thin red-haired boy
on the playing field. A shadow
that slammed him from behind,
a boot sliding down his instep
to freeze the muscle, bring numbness
and hollow pain. Breath in his ear:
How's that for a dead leg? Then tears
as he stood, unable to run away
or follow. A screen of daylight.

Fifty years later, this hotel room.
Empty bottles on the shelves
where his books had once been.
The TV, never switched off.
And sometimes, there were people:
admirers of a writer he'd forgotten,
drinking companions. He gave them
books and whiskey. They gave him
their faces to mask his ghosts.

And in the night, his dead leg
spoke to him as it blackened.
Its breath smelt of old leaves,
a lost garden, roses and briars.
On a table by the dark window,
the typewriter slept in its hood.
His leg whispered its stories.

Eventually, they cut it off.
He was dead a year later.

Back Room

To get started here, you have to be
too drunk to finish.

The air's thin with amyl nitrite,
and the shapes of hunger

are more visible, at first,
than the forest of silent men.

This where our dreams go
to hide, and dream of hiding.

The music drowns every voice.
The options of hunger are few:

kneel, close your dulled eyes,
touch the lines of a face,

feel a hand in your hair,
lick sap from the branches.

And afterwards, there's nothing
to do but walk on.

The stories are over,
but they cannot end:

I'll meet you by the river
where the gods are rotting.

Unrest

Ten years on, I dreamt
that you came back to my flat
in the small hours, tired and cold.
Outside, the fighting continued,

but you lay still in my arms.
For shelter, not for passion.
I held you until the dawn
and your eyes didn't close.

Below Zero

You can't freeze vodka
in a low-grade freezer.
It gets thick, viscous,
but there's no ice.

In an expensive freezer,
vodka becomes crystal.
Hard. It bites your hand,
won't melt in your mouth.

Chunks of iced vodka
drift through your blood
as if in the Antarctic.
They attach to your bones

and, layer by layer,
replace them. Permanent:
a skeleton of frozen
vodka. It will never

corrode, age or thaw.
An intimate fossil.
You could get drunk
just thinking about it.

Don't Soak the Fuse

Just a little thing, really. A spark.
Then the angry fizzing of light, its
drops blackening the grass,
the screaming comet, the horny
exploding sun, the peacock's eye
watching you over the rooftops.

It won't dare to rain until the show's
over. No messing. Just wait.

Light the blue touch paper and stand back.

Such a little spark. The night
is holding its breath. Counting.
All day I've felt it coming on.
All evening, sat here, turning the blade
in one hand. As thin as paper.

Look, its handwriting is red.
Like a spark. Don't cut too deep,
don't soak the fuse in petrol.

I watch the light spread across
the blade: fluid, dazzling. Then
look up at the corporate sky.
Rain all you fucking want. I'm smiling.

Bright Eye, Dark Eye

The one eye is a gem. A ballet dancer
with wings, on ice. A sparkling drink
like Diamond White with no aftertaste.
A summer day crushed like tinfoil,
revolving over a golden dancefloor

all night. The other eye is a hole.
Viscous. Toxic with unlet tears.
No light, no mirror, no shared glance
on that side of things. From the one,
you expect laughter. From the other,

silence. But you don't want the mind
that holds them together, the person
living in between. Just the eyes.
That's why I'm leaving, I'm getting
out of here. This way. No, this way.

City Reservoir

The ice glints in the sodium haze.
Through a fabric of splinters
I see dark figures trapped below,
struggling, dying, coming apart;
and the ice is thick under my feet,
but when I reach down to touch it
it's as thin, porous and easy
to cut as my own skin.

More figures are reaching out,
as if they wanted to save me
or needed me to save them.
If I could see the stars
they'd say we'll all be fine.
In my hand there's a script for ice.

Canal

I know where I start and end.
There's no need for movement.
Over the years, so many people
have dropped their furniture in me.
It rots gradually, a model home.
Parts of me sit on broken chairs,
stretch out on a bed of springs.
My belly is full of rust flakes
like the dust behind a window.
My skin has drunk the sour rain.
Don't expect me to take you
anywhere new. But sit here
for a while, and I'll show you
my collection of one photograph.

Second Draft

Yes, I'm talking to you.
See that door? Go on, open it
and then close it behind you.
Oh, and take all your stuff.
I'm sick of clearing up
after you: the bottles, the shoes,
the stale atmosphere of jokes
that weren't funny the first time.
Go to where you don't exist.
Where the rain slants through you,
and your shadow on the window
is a stranger's vacant face.
I'm sick of hearing your rants,
your promises, of apologising
for all the things you said.
Go and debate with an echo.
Go and sculpt a nude archangel
on some barren cloud. Go and play
with Metallica or with matches.
Go with anyone who asks.
Leave your suitcases in a quarry,
leave your footmark in the snow,
leave this minute. It's all over.
Go to jail. Do not pass Go.
When the wind burns the trees
and fingers the brittle newspaper,
stay away. When the snow melts
and freezes, bruising the stone,
and the legendary drinkers
who've never forgotten you
turn brittle on the inside, like
the singers in a glass choir,
don't get in touch. Come back
when something is different.
Come back in good time. Come back
in peace. Or don't ever come back.

The Real Him

You have to make allowances.
The odd remark off the cuff,
a joke or a quick flash of rage.

Just the way he was brought up.
Things were different. He'll never
expect you to agree with him.

It's a test of friendship
when he knocks on your door:
will you help him wash

the strange blood from his shirt
when he's shaking, unable to speak,
and you look and he's not hurt?

Contact Tracing

And after the songs of midnight
that struck flame from stony hearts,
after the low-key club tours, the late-
night TV concerts, the awards,

after the groupies, the smack,
the branding, the ménage à several,
the heart-to-heart in the Sunday paper,
after all of that, he came back

to the forest gate, the dark stairs,
the mine where the ghosts waited
unsleeping. Came back for you,
for that kiss, that melancholy walk

among the stone faces, the reek
of silence, to the polluted river
where he turned again, reached out
his thin arms to hold you back.

Spell

Walking up Salisbury Road as the lights come on
I can feel the sky, a blue felt blanket,

closer to my skin than the buildings
or the silhouettes of fresh-leaved trees,

and balanced on the roadway's ledge
I know why the witches said 'sky-clad'

instead of 'naked'; I'm reeling, drunk
on nothing but the colour of twilight.

After the Fire

It's not just a photograph. Step
here, between the blackened trees.
Turn a leaf to a smear on your hand.
Branches shatter when you press them,
reveal layers of dead skin.

The burnt world is easily reached.
You've worked on it all your life,
redrafting its silence, charring
your fruit to stock its orchards.
You watched the houses catch fire

and inhaled the bitter smoke.
You scattered a vase full of ash
on the dull water of its canals,
were respectful of the dead
even as the planes took flight.

Did the end justify the means?
This world is its own archive,
its own reversed fossil. Go on,
look for yourself. This is where you
belong. But don't expect company.

Common Ground

The Healing Begins

That first note cracks the still air.
A man is a hangover, a dull
smudge peering through itself
in the mirror. No sound is whole.
The machines are already turning,

but you can't put your slow hand
to any wheel. You're on a different
kind of shift, from blue to grey,
like a girder, a razor. Like dust.
This emptiness crowds the room.

You light a fire under creased foil,
watch the blue smoke that evades
your mouth, like a true word.
You can't even belong to the night.
Daybreak is a wrinkled sheet

of paper, a contract, a confession,
and all you can do is sign. Being
dead won't get you off the hook.
The melody cries out. You stand.
There's nothing left now but work.

A Vinyl Landscape

You don't come here often. It's a shrine
where your movements are guided, alone.
No grain of space is wasted: the records
packed so tight that your own hand

leaves them disordered, however hard
you try to replace them; the walls tiled
with rare albums in plastic sleeves,
the only windows this room has.

Browsing, you cross yourself as a student:
the records you thought *Must buy that
some day* are found only here; not cheap.
To touch the dried hand of the past

will always cost you. It draws you back
into childhood: the cold vinyl flooring;
the first plastic, not yet called *plastic*.
These records play only in real time.

For a few crumpled notes, you purchase
another soul or two; leave with a knot
of darkness in the back of your neck.
Sometimes you leave them wrapped for weeks

before kneeling to unwind the black
spiral groove, the thread in the labyrinth,
its dust fixed and ready to sing.
You make believe that the dead are here;

but wherever they are, it's another shelf,
records we don't have a means to play.
Perhaps there is only silence, the crackles
of the run-out groove, © John Cage

or a needle that's lost the will to lift.
You dream: *When I am too worn
for anything to extract a sound,
I want an urn made from vinyl.*

Dry Rain

It was over before anyone knew
it was happening. A hail of bullets
like nails released from a shell,
two bodies still on the pavement.
The car drove on. In the winter
frost always has the last word.

The Home Secretary made a list
of records he intended to ban,
none of which he'd ever heard;
then went back to planning a war
that would be over before anyone knew
or could photograph the torn bodies.

The cries will not be recorded.
A dry rain vomits from the sky,
from the radio, from your own throat,
and won't take words for an answer.
A dry hand tightens its grip
and the common ground is frozen.

Not Until Morning

Rain had polished the streets, turned them
to gold. We caught a taxi from the club
after a dance, some quiet talk. Halfway
to my flat, you started to shake, then
put a hand to your mouth. *Stop the car,*
my friend's sick. I opened the door. You
fell out onto the pavement.

short circuit   loose wire   a spark
jumping the gap   exposed nerve

For ten minutes, I held your head
to stop you cracking it open.
Your face was shining with tears
and saliva – your black hair slicked
over your pale forehead. *I wanted*
to hold you tonight, but not like this.
They trussed you like a cold chicken.

inertia   a terrible false sleep   eyes
open, but no movement   no words

Three hours in casualty, watching you
shudder and puke and cry out. Then
you slept. I left my number
with the charge nurse, walked out into
the night, the anticlimax of dawn
that left me scanning the white clouds
for the darkness pressing behind them.

poise   the dancer   a stillness
around you   the mimicry of calm

The first thing you'd said on coming to:
"Get me out of here." *Not until morning,*
I'd answered. They phoned me up then
to say, *He's well. Come and get him.*
I took you back to your flat, the prison
of its blank walls, the cell of your eyes.
"I have to move on. Now. But where?"

*three cities   your bitten accent   white
smoke   a face coming apart   reforming*

Between the Stars

Reality is a crutch for those
unable to cope with science fiction.
Space travel is now impossible

due to the rocket and satellite debris
orbiting the planet at random,
like pieces of a broken shell

around a slowly decaying egg.
Still, they've updated their hardware.
They sit over pints of real ale,

exchanging karaoke futurist quips.
The groove has worn too deep,
the twelve-bar blues impossible

to break. Every year their beards
are a little greyer, their stomachs a little
more pregnant with boredom.

The Prison Ship

We've seen them on the staircase
holding hands, heard the whisper
of their private conversation
echoing in the narrow corridor.

They smile whenever their paths cross.
Can't they feel the harbour's rhythm,
or does it make them think of love?
Can't they smell the decay from below?

Doesn't the salt breath of the wind
dry out their little hearts, cure them?
Don't they hear the anchor chain
groaning under its flesh of slime?

The day they leave, we'll turn back
to avoid hearing their struggle
as the black water closes over them
like a duvet, rocking them to sleep.

The Floor Show

Maybe we'd given the bed too much work
or maybe the boards were always rotten,
but either way, we fell without knowing

and now we're stuck between floors
in the insulation cavity, feeling the pipes
conduct their mournful conversation

around and between us, and dead things
trapped in the contact we used to share
more privately. But the rotting cables

jolt us back out of sleep, our dusty eyes
scratched by the light, our limbs tangled,
feeling we don't know what, but something.

Andromeda

Just around the corner, still here,
the shuttered room that was a bookshop.
The petrol-tinged air carries
no smell of paper, no secret
confirmation of the twenty years
I walked home from here, reading.

Without the stories, this city is
a prison. The light is blotchy,
a bad skin over the darkness.
The streets are paved with newsprint.
My hands grip the air, try
to mimic the shape of a book.

Where are they now? At home
or pacing the streets? Their eyes cold
and staring from lack of dreams.
For a moment, through the torn-up clouds,
I can see the faint swirl of a galaxy
frozen, a snapshot made permanent.

Note: Andromeda Bookshop has since re-opened in new premises.

The Ghost Market

The bus skirts its fenced-off edge:
a red crater in the concrete ground,
marked by the teeth of JCBs.

Deeper than any burial pit,
as deep as a new foundation.
This cloaca has dropped the sky.

Caught in the centre, between
shut-down book and record shops,
I feel the breath of the Bull Ring pit;

and the worst things I have said
float around me like razor-wire.
We've buried our words in the ground,

but there's no need to dig them up.
Spoken by the damp wind, they
will never be silent – just as

it's never silent in the city centre:
there's a litter of sounds and voices
that no-one can quite pick up.

Days of 1979

By the time we came along, dragging
our parents' battle-flags like satchels,
the excitement was pretty much over.

I remember a girl who slashed her blazer
so she could refuse to wear it.
We had no ideals to live up to

except sarcasm, disbelief and rejection.
In retrospect, those were ideals –
which says a lot about later on.

I remember walking on my own
in the greater loneliness of the tribes –
Rastas, punks, mods, rockers, skins –

a sadness that transcended conflict
like a glance across a barren playground,
and told us all the future would stink.

I was only just too young
to vote when Thatcher came to power.
Punk changed music, but nothing else.

I found a hymn in the jagged pulse
of despair, the bands shrouded in black
like the shadow of a great fire.

A Neat Bloodstain

As a child you dreamed of the house
burning, and woke to find
your nose had bled on the pillow.
Small marks, like cigarette burns.

You never dreamed of oceans
or beating wings. Forty years driving
on the same narrow roads. All
your best ideas were turned down.

Even when you cut yourself, it only
bled for a short while. Now, lying
on a hospital bed, you could cough
your heart out and not make a mess.

Chorus

A pale assembly of candles,
a megaphone leading a chant.

A tabloid of revolution,
posters gutted by the rain.

They march along the same route,
but will they stand together

with the shreds of a torn flag
resembling one common wound?

There doesn't seem much chance,
now the deviant Pied Piper

has taken all the children away
and left us with these innocents.

The Ruined City

Now that you've wasted your life here, in this small corner,
you've destroyed it everywhere in the world.
                                                    — C.P. Cavafy

Always, in those yellowed travel stories,
it was the myth the explorers found
hidden in the fever-swamp or the cold waste:
a city older than humanity, webbed

with cracks and tendrils, no wall intact.
And buried in these elaborate ruins,
something precious or something evil,
human or alien: a secret horror.

As a child, you made the streets around you
a ruined city, peopled with the dead.
Its hidden secret kept you safe,
insured you against loss or knowledge.

A lifetime has to speed up decay,
pour dust by the vanload
between the cracks. There's no other way
to get the smell of the eternal

into your mouth. You were young
when the ruins flowered, the grey
spores of rust and broken glass.
Lost and ecstatic like the traveller,

you couldn't get away. The ruined city
enclosed you, made you its secret.
You sat by the dead phone, crying,
scribbling runes of enlightenment

on the back of an unpaid bill.
It takes a kind of faith to see
failure in everything, and faith
can end. A thousand years

or a decade, it's the same thing.
Around you, the shattered buildings
started to heal. And the staring dead
wiped the dust from their eyes

and became people you knew,
who left the imprints of their fingers
and mouths on your exposed face.
And the voice that had said *Too late*

murmured, *So what happens next?*
You turned the blank page, and knew
that what you'd read as destruction
was just a form of architecture.

Echoland

The music weaves back over itself,
not blurring; each still note
echoes and never fades away.

The phrases are coils of smoke
drifting from silver paper,
hardening into ice sculptures

the sun will never melt.
If you can touch this landscape,
be part of it, you'll never leave.

Can you walk away from perfection?
Fucking hell, you'd better. Then
a lifetime passes between tracks.

Don't Go

You said, stone dies like us.
They knocked down that pub
off Deritend, close to the viaduct
that'll be the next thing to go.
I said, but stone doesn't live:

just sweats it day after day,
holding on, but not feeling,
slowly growing a coat of ash
while the lime drips from its pores.
You said, that's not living?

Biographical Note

Joel Lane lives in Birmingham, where he works as a free-lance editor and writer. He won an Eric Gregory award for poetry in 1993. His first collection of poems, *The Edge of the Screen*, was published by Arc in 1999. He is also author of two novels, *From Blue To Black* and *The Blue Mask* (Serpent's Tail) and a collection of short stories, *The Earth Wire* (Egerton Press). He has also edited an anthology of subterranean horror stories, *Beneath the Ground* (The Alchemy Press), and he and Steve Bishop have edited an anthology of crime and suspense stories *Birmingham Noir* (Tindal Street Press). He is currently working on his third novel, *Midnight Blue*.

Recent publications in
Arc Publications' series
POETRY FROM THE UK / IRELAND
edited by Jo Shapcott
include:

LIZ ALMOND
The Shut Drawer

JONATHAN ASSER
Outside The All Stars

DONALD ATKINSON
In Waterlight: Poems New, Selected & Revised

JULIA DARLING
Sudden Collapses in Public Places
Apology for Absence

CHRISSIE GITTINS
Armature

HERBERT LOMAS
The Vale of Todmorden

IAN POPLE
An Occasional Lean-to

SUBHADASSI
peeled

JACKIE WILLS
Fever Tree